1994

Mystique of the Missions

Mystique of the Missions

Photographic Impressions by

Marvin Wax

Descriptive Passages by Charles Francis Saunders and J. Smeaton Chase
Selected from *The California Padres and Their Missions*, published in 1915.

An IMAGES OF AMERICA SERIES book

AMERICAN WEST PUBLISHING COMPANY
PALO ALTO - CALIFORNIA

To my wife Beatrice
for her patient encouragement
and valuable artistic counsel.

Special Editor: Patricia Kollings

FIRST EDITION

© Copyright 1974, by AMERICAN WEST PUBLISHING COMPANY. Printed in the United States of America. All rights reserved. This book or parts thereof may not be reproduced in any form without written permission of the publisher.

Library of Congress Card Number 74-77396

ISBN: regular casebound edition, 0-910118-52-3; deluxe edition, 0-910118-53-1

Foreword

There is a strange mystique about the Spanish Missions of California that seems to be nearly as old as the adobe compounds themselves. They were still in their heyday when Alfred Robinson (*Life in California*) and Richard Henry Dana, Jr. (*Two Years Before the Mast*) visited them and were moved to tell the world of what they saw. Later in the nineteenth century, Victorian travelers marveled and wept over the decaying ruins of the padres' labors; Helen Hunt Jackson was so impressed that she wrote both a travelogue-history (*Father Junipero and the Mission Indians of California*) and a novel (*Ramona*) about them.

Nor have the massive restorations that most of the Missions have undergone in the last few decades stemmed the tide of admirers. In fact, today they come in greater numbers than ever, recording their delight with Nikons and Instamatics.

One of these visitors was professional photographer Marvin Wax, who shared all the ardor of the amateurs but brought along some rather rare artistic and technical skills as well. For several years, whenever an assignment brought him into the neighborhood of a Mission, he would steal a few hours to explore it. The result is the remarkable collection of photographs in this book.

Wax made no attempt at documentation but simply turned his camera on whatever touched his emotions. Avoiding sleekly restored areas, he sought out the bones of the original Missions—the crumbling walls, neglected gravestones, floor tiles hollowed by sandaled feet. These were the objects in front of his lens, but his real subject seems to have been Time. Time and its relation to the works of men—the gentle paradox by which, as it slowly, inexorably destroys man's structures and institutions, it often at the same time lends them a patina, a charm and beauty that exceed any they enjoyed in their prime.

Perhaps one reason that the artist in Wax was drawn to the Missions was that they provided such ideal material for the special techniques of lighting and color printing with which he has been experimenting. With natural, often diffused light sources, some of his photographs seem almost like paintings. Besides being aesthetically pleasing, this technique has proved to be a highly effective way of conveying his message about timelessness.

The pictures seem to us to stand on their own. They need no commentary to explain them. Instead, they are presented with a counterpoint of musical prose by two earlier observers, Charles Francis Saunders and J. Smeaton Chase, who visited the California Missions just after the turn of the century. In *The California Padres and Their Missions*, published in 1915, Saunders and Chase tell what they saw and how they felt about it in words as sensitive and unabashedly poetic as Wax's photographs.

Saunders was an American, a historian, and an afficionado of the Spanish Colonial period. Chase was an Englishman, an adoptive but devoted son of California, and a fine writer. There is no clue in *The California Padres* as to which passages were the voice of Saunders and which that of Chase, or whether, as one present-day authority has suggested, all were originally written by Saunders and then polished by Chase (thus accounting for the perceptible British flavor throughout the text).

It is not intended that the quotations serve as captions for the photographs. They were, after all, written more than a half century earlier. But their spirit is surprisingly similar—their authors even singled out some of the same scenes that moved Marvin Wax.

We hope that together words and photographs will guide the reader through a rewarding emotional and aesthetic experience, offering him new beauties to behold and familiar ones to see through fresh eyes, giving expression for him to the feelings of delight he may have felt himself under the spell of the Missions.

PATRICIA KOLLINGS

$\mathcal{I}$t was autumn, still dry and dusty, and the sun was high; and, as I walked through a glory of wild sunflowers and across barley stubble, my feet released terebinthine incense from blue curls and tarweed. . . . By and by I passed a great shallow reservoir of masonry, obviously Mission-made, and then some juisache trees (the Acacia farnesiana, whose fragrant balls of fluffy bloom were beloved of the Padres). Then came a little forest of tuna cactus, and a crumbling adobe wall, and along the last, a dusty path brought me to the Mission.

I passed through a wicket into the arcaded corridor, . . .

. . . which chairs, a bench or two, roses clambering about the pillars, and a flowery array of potted plants had transformed into a delightful outdoor living room.

The cool corridor, with its worn, echoing pavement of <u>ladrillos</u>; the square brick pillars stained and broken by Time into greater beauty, I suspect, than they possessed in their spick-and-span youth; and the outlook through the arches and the fringe of locust trees to the peaceful plaza and beyond—these were altogether lovely.

The architecture is all very interesting
and marvelous...

...when one remembers the work was done in a remote
wilderness under the direction of a couple of Friars
by Indian workmen who shortly before were as wild and
untrained as plover.

The quaint mouldings about doors and windows,

and the delightful handwrought <u>rejas</u> of iron,

the work doubtless of neophyte masons and blacksmiths...

—all this was material for the artistic soul.

An open door led to a boxlike vestibule within, at the end of
which was a closed door and in it a little window such as ticket
offices have. . . .

I gently touched the bell.

The sacristan led me a rapid march through the garden, really a charming nook, of which I should have liked to see more, with a modern palm tree or two, an arbored walk where vines of Mission grapes cast a meditative shade, and the perfume of roses sweetened the air.

15 31, 448

All about were old-fashioned flowers blowing perfume across my path and ducking their pretty heads at me as the breeze passed over them ...

...while on each side of the shadow-dappled walk,

and set at regular intervals in the shade of the olives,

were little wooden shrines, each lovingly clasped by

a twining rose.

In Mission days cattle by the tens of thousands fed upon

the bordering plains ... and were slaughtered daily for

their hides and tallow. This shipping of these hides was

a picturesque sight. The Indians in long files, each carrying

a golded skin on his head, wound through the wild mustard

to the <u>embarcadero</u>, where the hides were dumped into lighters

for the port of San Francisco.

So productive were the San Gabriel lands and so genial
the climate that this Mission has been called the Mother
of Agriculture in California...though the land was
prepared...by merely scratching with a wooden plough
made often of the forked limb of a tree, shod at the point
with a flat piece of iron, and drawn by oxen.

Underground, I was shown a great adobe wine vat—a sort of Mission version of the Great Tun of Heidelberg . . .

. . . and the cellar where, I suppose, the stock
of wine and aguardiente was stored to mellow—
that far-famed vintage of San Fernando which, the
ancient encomium went, was "as the smile of
Providence."

As I strolled about, I came here and there upon reservoirs and other remains of the fine irrigation system. . . .

. . . One strongly built basin had steps
of square red tiles descending into it, as
though for the convenience of Indians going
down to wash their clothing in the water
there, or perhaps for [Mission] Rebeccas
to fill their jars the more easily.

Turning into an echoing inner corridor, we came

to a small courtyard, two sides of it new and sleek,

but one, thank Heaven, still as of yore with its

time-stained, broken plaster; . . . and an ancient

fountain still remained in the midst. . . .

...For an hour I loitered about in quiet undisturbed,
except for the scratching of a rake in the hands
of a Brother at work among his roses and callas in
the garden of the larger patio adjoining, and the
occasional footfalls of some other Brother as he
pattered along the inside corridors.

$\mathcal{A}$t every turn some charming bit of handiwork catches
the eye. There are handwrought shelves fixed, immovable,
in the thick adobe walls; wall pockets scooped deep
in the adobe; ...

...hand-hewn ceiling beams, and snug joinery
without nails; scrolls and designs of simple
beauty worked into doorposts and lintels; and
delightful moldings about the doorways...

—*doorways so low that even a short man must humble himself to pass through.*

A dark-skinned señora opened to me, and I asked if I might see within. Her knowledge of English seemed limited to "Please, ten cents." I paid it willingly enough and we prepared for the adventure as if for a visit to a cave, a lantern being selected from a dozen on the table, lighted, and placed in the hands of a pretty little barefoot damsel who would act as my guide.

Her name, Consuelo Valenzuela, was like a strain of music,
and indicated membership in an old Spanish-Californian
family. She led the way through the various rooms, giving
me such scraps of information as she knew, which was not much.

All was bare to the bone, and of various degrees of darkness, in some the windows being boarded up tight to keep out intruders.

One was known to have been the Padres' refectory; in another, some gaping cracks in the wall betokened the temblor's visitation.

The relics have been patiently got together from all sorts of places—from the cluttered corners of the Missions ruins, from crumbling outhouses, from the earth of the surrounding fields as the plough turns it up, from the garrets of the countryside, from city junk shops.

There were beautiful old basins and cups and kettles

of hammered copper; crucifixes of wood wonderfully and

realistically carved, some with a cord, meaning that

the carver was a Franciscan; and there was a quaint

wooden <u>metraca</u> like a watchman's rattle, for use at

the altar in Holy Week when bells are stilled.

There were wooden candlesticks with carved and painted ornamentations; and ...

...there were great parchment books with

manuscript church music written by monkish hands

now turned to dust; ...

...and there was a desk full of manuscript Mission records bound in skin, the covers fastened with buckskin ties...done in the careful script of a day when leisure was no disgrace.

A cheerful little old woman of housekeeperly aspect...
ushered me into the cool twilight of the church. The interior
proved very attractive. The old square-brick tiling of the floor
was worn into hollows and humps by the tread of generations, and
the walls were elaborately decorated in the primitive style
and gaudy tones that bore evidence of Indian artists having
contributed largely to the adornment. There was a charming
old wall pulpit with a sounding board suspended above it like
a candle extinguisher about to drop; ... and an ancient
wood ceiling, supported by hewn timber beams. ...

...*The altar was adorned with a painted wooden statue of the Archangel, and over him a huge sunlike carving of gilded wood, radiating gilt spokes, symbolized, I believe, the omnividency of God. All this, in the half light from an occasional little window well up under the roof, was as an old Mission should be.*

A feature of the Mission is the cemetery, . . . a weedy, tangled, down-at-the-heel cemetery, with the tombs and headstones at all angles, yet, in a way, more eloquent of the past than the taciturn old church; for every headstone tells a story.

A neatly barbered, right-angled <u>camposanto</u> would be more respectful to the buried, I suppose; but somehow the half-wild tangle of this, with its unkempt malva roses, its unrestrained myrtle wandering in gypsy freedom over rail and walk,... seems quite in keeping with the patriarchal, pastoral California, contemporaneous with the old Mission.

The ramshackle wooden crosses stagger wildly on the shapeless mounds; the dilapidated whitewashed railings, cracked and blistered by the sun, look much as though they might be bleached bones, tossed carelessly about; and the badly painted, misspelled inscriptions yield up their brief announcements only to a very patient reader.

Roofless...and half hidden in a tangle of wild mustard and rank weeds, [the church] is desolate as Tadmor in its wilderness, and seemingly as thoroughly beyond hope of repair.

It stands in its devastation a temple eloquent with
the gospel of beauty, the stars its candles, the birds
of the air its choristers.

What remains is a rambling ruin of ... mudbrick walls, broken and breached by the elements, strolling cattle, and graceless humanity; and every year puts them but farther on their Avernian road....

...I passed within and, picking my way over rubbish
heaps of broken tiles and collapsed walls, sat down on
a mound of melted mudbricks to think it over....

...A rabbit, startled at the unwonted noise of footsteps, leaped from its home amid the dusty debris where I fancied the ancient altar had been, and scuttled away. A ground owl chittered in the neighboring fields, and I could see him atop of his sticks of legs, ridiculously bowing at nothing. By and by a quail out there called. Then unbroken stillness.

Acknowledgments

Marvin Wax and the editors wish to express their warmest appreciation to all of those people who contributed in one way or another to the creation of this book: to Harry Downie, Richard H. Dillon, Lawrence C. Powell, and Richard G. Lillard for sharing their knowledge of the Missions and their chroniclers; to the staffs of the various Missions for their gracious assistance and permission to photograph; and to Norman Shapiro for his help and companionship through the many months of photography.

Photographic Notes

It seems as though I have been concerned with seeing—really seeing—since I was very young. When I was just a child in grade school, I had the good fortune to be patted on the back for my drawing efforts and directed toward a career in art. In those days I was sketching portraits of movie stars (I have a vivid recollection of one of Claudette Colbert), and I can still hear the words of encouragement that my sixth grade teacher gave me. This early guidance and encouragement led to my acceptance at the Cooper Union Institute in New York City, where I received a broad and thorough indoctrination into the arts. Upon graduation I went into commercial art and for the next fifteen years worked as a designer in advertising.

All this was a helpful background for photography, but it was not until about ten years ago that I first took a camera in hand, and only in the last five have I become really serious about it as an art form. To be serious about something is to love what you are doing. I have always been sensually oriented—very conscious of what I am seeing, smelling, touching, and hearing—and I find photography enables me to record my response to a scene quickly.

What attracted me to the California Missions? I am not sure. Maybe it was my love for antiques, with their painstaking, handcrafted construction. The Missions *are* antiques, weathered and deteriorated by Time. They offer an opportunity to look at the world of 1771 more than two hundred years later.

Or perhaps it's a matter of color—I think I am primarily a colorist (I say "think" because every day photography brings a photographer new understanding of himself). Time has done beautiful things to the color of the adobe brick walls. Like old people, the Missions have their history etched in color and line on their faces.

The photographs in this book were taken over a period of two and a half or three years. I did not have a precise plan or schedule but simply photographed the Missions on weekends, or whenever other business put me on Highway 101. Not until recently did I think of publishing my material.

A trip to a Mission didn't always mean that I would photograph. Many hours were spent just carrying my equipment around and looking. When I didn't photograph, was it because I wasn't seeing or because there was nothing to see? I don't know. Other times the light seemed exciting and alive. I couldn't shoot fast enough. Was it because *I* was excited and alive that day?

The process of seeing and photographing is exhausting, and after a while fatigue and inspiration begin to fight each other. For that reason I strongly resist carrying more weight than necessary. I like to save my energy for seeing and taking pictures. I have two Nikkormat 35mm camera bodies with three Nikkor lenses—28mm, 50mm, and 105mm. They did all the work in this book, and very seldom did I feel the need for more equipment.

Weight is one of the reasons I prefer to work with available light rather than carrying flood or flash equipment with me. However, I also love the soft quality that indirect natural light gives a picture. My early photographs of the Missions were all exteriors, usually taken on hazy or overcast days rather than in bright sunshine. For a long time I resisted working inside the Missions because the available light was so minimal. (Some Mission officials frown on the photographing of interiors, partly because strong light can deteriorate ancient books and vestments. I generally speak to the person in charge, tell him why I am there, and ask his permission to take pictures.) As I began to experiment, I found that by using long exposures, I could photograph inside without supplementary light. In fact, given enough time, the film will pick up even details that the eye does not see in the same light. The only problem with these long exposures is that the color tends to shift toward the yellows.

All of the pictures in this book were taken with Kodachrome II. I like its color and grainless emulsion. Its slow speed does not concern me since most of the time my camera is on a tripod. That way I can compose more carefully and am assured of minimal camera movement and maximum image sharpness.

In the end there seems to be an element of luck in photography. Several things have to get together—the photographer's mood, the subject, and the light. If all three are right at the same time, one has a good chance of making a good photograph. I have revisited some of the Missions several times. Often I go back to a spot where I took a great picture on an earlier visit, but it never looks so great the second time. Moments don't repeat themselves. My mood, the subject, and the light are never quite the same the second time. At the Missions the subject may have completely disappeared; a mellow old wall may have been covered with fresh paint or a broken cross carted away to the dump. I am always glad that I caught the one precious moment while I could.

Photographic Details

Jacket and Page 2: Belfry at Carmel Mission. Both pictures were the result of a couple of hours of observation and familiarization, primarily to observe the angle of the sun's light and its effect on surface detail. A 28mm lens was used for the jacket shot, a 50mm for page 2. I used an aperture setting of *f*22 to achieve a maximum depth of field.

Page 9: Doorway at San Juan Bautista. I used a 105mm lens because of its comparatively narrow angle of view, which enabled me to isolate the wanted information.

Page 11: Courtyard at San Juan Capistrano. This photograph is one of the few in the book taken in bright sunlight —the tranquility of the scene at that moment was irresistible. Using a wide-angle 28mm lens, I was able to capture the maximum architectural detail with a minimum of vertical convergence.

Page 13: Courtyard at San Juan Capistrano. This photograph was taken several minutes before the one on page 11. The sun hadn't quite pierced the morning fog. The light was softer and for me much more compatible with the subject. I worked with a frenzy, knowing that the harsh sun would soon break through. Also taken with my 28mm lens.

Page 15: Belfry and wall, San Gabriel Mission. Taken with a 50mm lens.

Page 16: Outer corridor at San Juan Capistrano. Corridors like this one, so typical of the Missions, make one feel sheltered yet not confined. 28mm lens.

Page 17: Pillar, San Juan Capistrano. As a photograph, this simple column detail has as much import as the many complete archways on page 16. 50mm lens.

Page 19: Doorway at Santa Barbara. To me this photograph typifies my response to the Missions and perhaps says why I photographed them. The doorway is a fascinating architectural detail, made more interesting by the light, virtually nondirectional, that bounced from surrounding walls. I used a long 105mm lens to maximize the flat design and texture.

Page 20: Window at San Juan Capistrano. The brownish-green color of this subject and the visual incongruity of the religious scene behind the window intrigued me. 28mm lens.

Page 22: Sculpture at San Antonio Mission. I was attracted to this weathered wooden figure that refused to give up its life and vitality. 50mm lens.

Page 23: Wooden madonna and child, sculptured by Indian hands at Carmel. I love the patina and color of this aging wood. 50mm lens.

Page 25: Statue of St. Francis in the garden at Carmel. This statue and the lighting on the entire scene generate a very mystical feeling for me. (The branch is not in St. Francis's hand, as it appears to be at first glance, but is part of the garden in the background.) 50mm lens.

Page 27: Cannas at San Luis Obispo. There was a pleasing contrast of texture between the soft red petals and the hard background tile, yet both are weathering and giving in to Time. To isolate the flowers and the tile from the surrounding details, I used a 105mm lens.

Page 29: Statue of the Virgin at Mission Dolores. Photographed in the fascinating light reflected from a late afternoon sky. 50mm lens.

Page 30: Barrel cactus. Like many other cacti, this plant is compatible with Missions and hot, arid country. I zeroed in close with a 105mm lens.

Page 31: Imprint of cross on tree bark at San Miguel. Apparently a crucifix was once nailed to the trunk of this tree. When after many years it was removed, it left a different but perhaps more potent cross imagery in its place. 105mm lens.

Page 32: Hide on fence at Purissima Mission, where cattle once roamed the far-flung Mission lands. 28mm lens.

Page 35: Wooden cart in field near Purissima Mission. 28mm lens.

Page 36: Water purifier at Purissima. This structure served to filter water as it flowed down from the hills. I had to walk a good distance from the Mission to find this scene. The late afternoon sun was moving in and out of clouds, and bees moved in and out of the wildflowers. It seemed that all of Nature was there—and me. 50mm lens.

Page 37: Arrastra at San Antonio Mission. In early times animals were hitched to the horizontal, revolving post—I imagined that I could still see them walking in circles, grinding corn, and going nowhere. 28mm wide-angle lens.

Page 38: Vat of handmade adobe bricks at San Juan Capistrano. This particular vat is round and was used for tallow making. The wine vat at San Fernando, described by Saunders and Chase, was of similar construction but square. The nuances of color and the play of light here intrigued me, and although it was underground, I was able to capture it with a time exposure. 50mm lens.

Page 40: Wheel of wine press at San Luis Obispo. 105mm lens.

Page 41: Wine bottle in window at San Antonio de Padua, one of my favorite Missions. I love the broad reflected daylight coming through the window. When I took this picture, there was an eerie quiet, with dust and spiders spinning their webs and a strong suggestion of time gone by. 50mm lens.

Page 43: Tile steps to the reservoir at San Luis Rey. The day was warm and pleasant, but I wished the sun had been a bit softer. These were a lot of steps, all of handmade tile. To dramatize that, I used my 28mm lens.

Page 45: Brick water trough at San Luis Rey. The steps on page 43 led to this trough. There was water moving slowly in the foreground, and I noticed little minnows by the hundreds swimming under the fallen and decayed leaves. The constant presence of water had encouraged slippery moss to cling to the bricks, and I didn't chance standing on them. 28mm lens.

Page 48: Tree roots and arches at San Juan Capistrano. The Mission buildings seem a lot like this great old tree— both have their roots deep in the soil and both speak of the passing of time. Photographed from ground level with a 28mm lens.

Page 50: Original roof tiles at San Miguel. These tiles were at shoulder level, enabling me to photograph them straight on. I moved intimately close and put my camera on a tripod to ensure stability; one-half second exposure at ƒ8 with a 50mm lens.

Page 51: Statue of St. Benedict in wall niche at Carmel. This figure caught my attention because of its strong, elegantly simple form. I preferred a straight-on, almost two-dimensional result, so I stood back about 30 feet with my 105 mm lens on a tripod.

Page 53: Stairway leading to the bell tower at San Luis Obispo. This area had a dank smell, but I loved what I saw. The soft light pouring in from the left illuminated the aging texture and gave subtleties to the color. 28mm lens.

Page 55: Low doorway at Santa Inez. This is one of my favorite pictures. Unfortunately, the scene no longer exists —the second time I returned, I found the walls replastered. Restoration destroys the æsthetic value for me, and today the subject would no longer demand my attention. I could

not move back very far because of stationary objects in the way, so a wide-angle 28mm lens was necessary.

Page 57: Carved wood door with iron pull at Santa Inez. Time does beautiful things to wood and metal. Photographed in late afternoon light with 50mm lens.

Page 59: Wall and bench at San Juan Capistrano. This photo is one of the few that I took with dazzling, directional light falling on the scene. It was late afternoon, and I had to hurry because the light was changing. 28mm lens.

Page 61: Interior at San Miguel. This scene shows how important lighting can be in creating the mood of a picture. 50mm lens.

Page 62: Dove on nest at San Juan Capistrano. All the birds at Capistrano aren't swallows. There were many birds around the Missions being hand fed by the visitors, so tame that they were easily photographed. It was late afternoon when this dove retired to its nest. (He may not have appreciated my intrusion.) I gently set my camera and tripod down, and he cooperated. The light was fading rapidly, and I had to hurry to get this shot. One second exposure at ƒ5.6 with 50mm lens.

Page 63: Barred window at San Juan Capistrano. I liked the strong light hitting the orange-toned wall. 28mm lens.

Page 64: Bucket and candle dipper at San Antonio. I revisited this Mission three times, and upon the last visit I became intrigued with this picture. The scene suggests a lot about the life and work of an earlier day. It was extremely dark, so I experimented with exposures of several seconds at ƒ5.6. In the end the Kodachrome film saw more than my eyes did. 50mm lens.

Page 67: Statue of St. Benedict at Carmel. St. Benedict seems to be a favorite subject of the early Indian woodcarvers. This statue was already split with age and was protected in a glass-enclosed case. I had to angle the camera carefully to avoid reflections in the glass. It was again extremely dark, so I used a five-second exposure at ƒ5.6 with a 105mm lens. The colors shifted somewhat toward the yellow side, but I don't think that detracts from the beauty of the picture.

Page 68: Close-up of the hands of a statue at Santa Cruz. Though the old Mission buildings at Santa Cruz have all disappeared, some of the original artifacts still are preserved in the church that was later built on the site. I like this picture—perhaps because I like hand gestures and the patina of wearing colors. It shows that sometimes a partial study can be as interesting as a complete study. 50mm lens.

Page 69: Feet of a statue of Our Lady of Mount Carmel at Carmel Mission. I was intrigued with the purples, blues, reds, and greens blended together with light. Though I knew immediately I had the makings of a good photograph, I worked for an hour composing it at every conceivable angle and with all three lenses. For this particular shot I used my 50mm.

Page 70: Candle and old manuscript at San Antonio. I would have liked to move these objects to improve the composition, but they were fragile and the signs said "Please don't touch." 50mm lens.

Page 73: Music manuscript at San Gabriel Mission. This manuscript was virtually hidden in darkness within a protective glass cabinet. Strong light of any kind has a deteriorating effect on color and materials. I recall using a five- or ten-second exposure at ƒ5.6. The lens was a 50mm, hand held, but I braced the camera against a wall for stability.

Page 75: Books at San Luis Rey. 50mm lens.

Page 77: Church nave at San Miguel. When I entered the church, it was quiet but the light was vibrating, illuminating the beautiful colors. I sat on one of the benches, slowly being absorbed into the past. After a long while I took this picture. 28mm lens.

Page 79: Pulpit at San Miguel. The soft interior light made the colors in this scene glow in a way that reminds me of some contemporary art expressions. 50mm lens.

Page 80: A 180-year-old statue of St. Bonaventure salvaged from the old Mission San Jose. I positioned my camera carefully to silhouette the dark-robed statue against the light wall. 28mm lens.

Page 81: Old harness on shelf at San Miguel. It is amazing what the camera can record. This photograph was taken in a dark, damp, mildewy corridor, but because of long exposure the film picked up more detail than my eye could see. 28mm lens.

Page 82: Doorway and daisies at San Juan Capistrano. 50mm lens.

Page 83: Two graves bordered with seashells at Carmel. The shells are standing the test of time, almost eternally resistant to the elements, while above and below them are reminders of man's perishability. 50mm lens.

Page 85: Crosses in the cemetery at San Juan Bautista. This day the light and a clear atmosphere cooperated with me. I crawled on my stomach to compose the picture in such a way that the crosses would be silhouetted against the sky. 28mm lens.

Page 86: Gravestone at Mission Dolores. It was the rainy season in San Francisco when I took this picture, and the leaves were saturated with water and color. Fallen as they were, they seemed to give the gravestone an unwritten message. I used my 105mm lens, hand held with tripodlike rigidity directly over the stone.

Page 87: Another gravestone at Mission Dolores. I like the way the sun starkly illuminates the spiky leaves against this dark, symmetrical gravestone. 105mm lens.

Page 88: Rose in a Mission garden. 50mm lens.

Page 89: Cross marking a grave at Mission Santa Inez. The cross was in unusual harmony with the background wall. I lay on my stomach to achieve a low angle of view and carefully positioned myself so the cross would delineate itself against the lighter part of the wall. Next time I returned to Santa Inez, the wall had been replastered—that image will never occur again. 105 mm lens, hand held.

Page 91: White wooden cross at Mission Santa Barbara. The cross, wall color, and texture all blend together in harmony. Several minutes later the sun pierced through with harsh overhead light. At that point, I walked away. 105mm lens.

Page 92: Headless statue at Santa Barbara. This picture has an absence of color, but I feel its monochromatic tone reveals one side of Mission history. 28mm lens.

Page 93: Broken cross at Mission Carmel. This was one of my first pictures and still is one of my favorites. Upon my third return to Carmel, the cross was no longer there. It made me sad. 28mm lens with a half-second exposure at ƒ5.6.

Page 94: Millstone at San Antonio. 28mm lens.

Page 95: Statue of the Virgin at San Juan Bautista. Time has given color to the adobe walls in this picture. 28mm lens.

Page 97: Ruined wall, discovered on my fourth visit to San Juan Bautista. Except for the protective fence, it could have been taken 150 years ago (if one had had the equipment). There was no way to shoot around the fence, so I included it in the composition. 28mm lens.

Page 98: Ruins at San Juan Capistrano. One can spend many days at this Mission photographing the adobe remains of the devastating 1812 earthquake. They are truly magnificent. For this picture I had to work quickly because the light was fading. 28mm lens.

Page 101: Fragment of an arch at Mission Santa Inez. It still stands proudly, thrusting its masonry into the sky.

There is a protective fence around this structure, too, which severely limited my mobility and vantage points. 28mm lens, hand held.

Page 103: Century plant and ruins at Mission Soledad. It was hot, windy, and lonely there amid the ruins. They were trying to withstand the elements but were slowly and inevitably eroding. Only the plant had life—the plant and I. 28mm lens.

Page 104: More ruins at Soledad. I was fascinated by the painstaking sculpting being done by the sun, rain, and wind upon the adobe structures. When it is complete, there will be nothing. 28mm lens.

1

Body type, Granjon, set by CBM Type, Mountain View, California; display initials, Bernhard Cursive, set by Typographic, San Francisco; display face, Fraktur, set by Paul O. Giesey/Adcrafters, Portland, Oregon. Printed by Graphic Arts Center, Portland.

Design by Dannelle Pfeiffer and Patricia Kollings